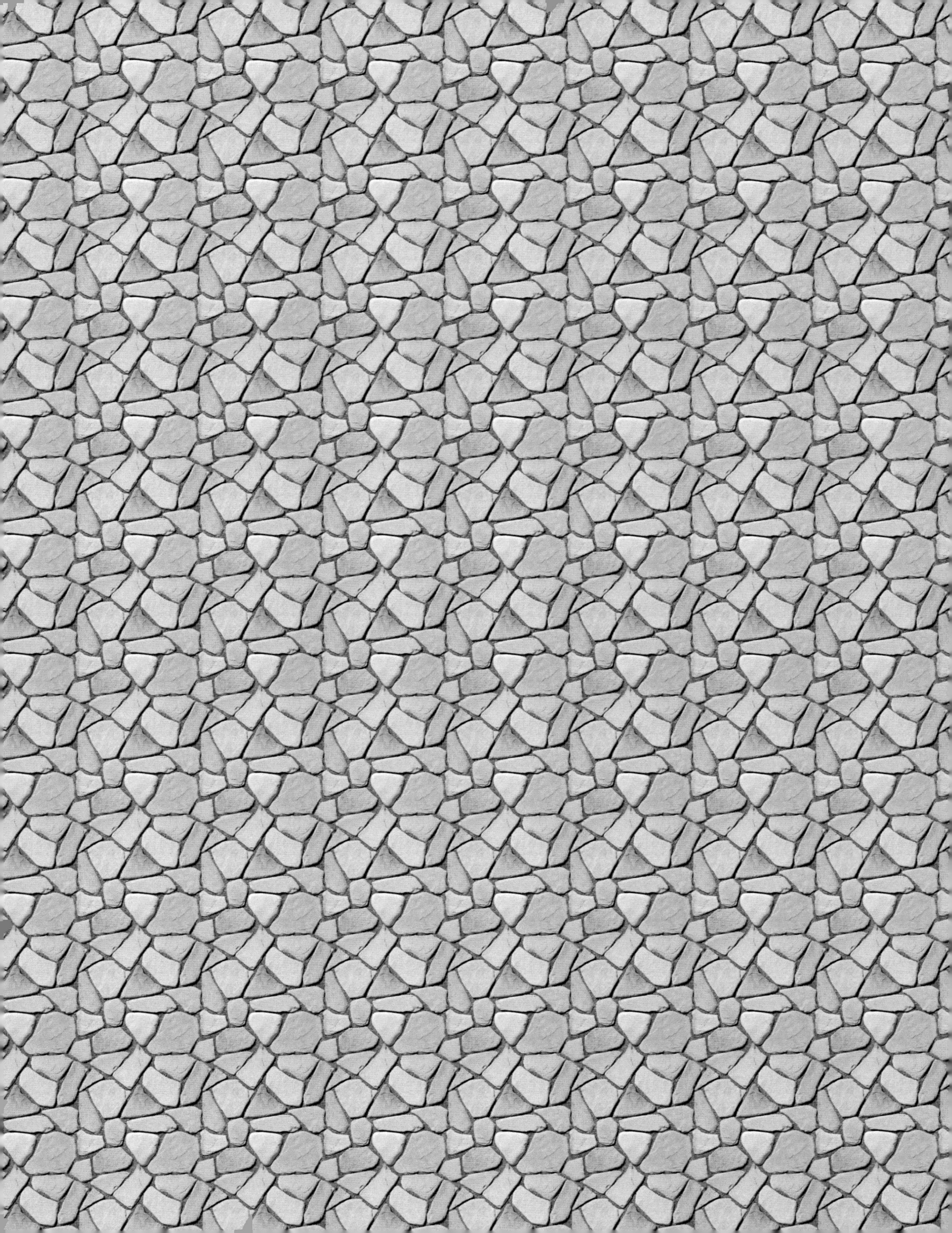

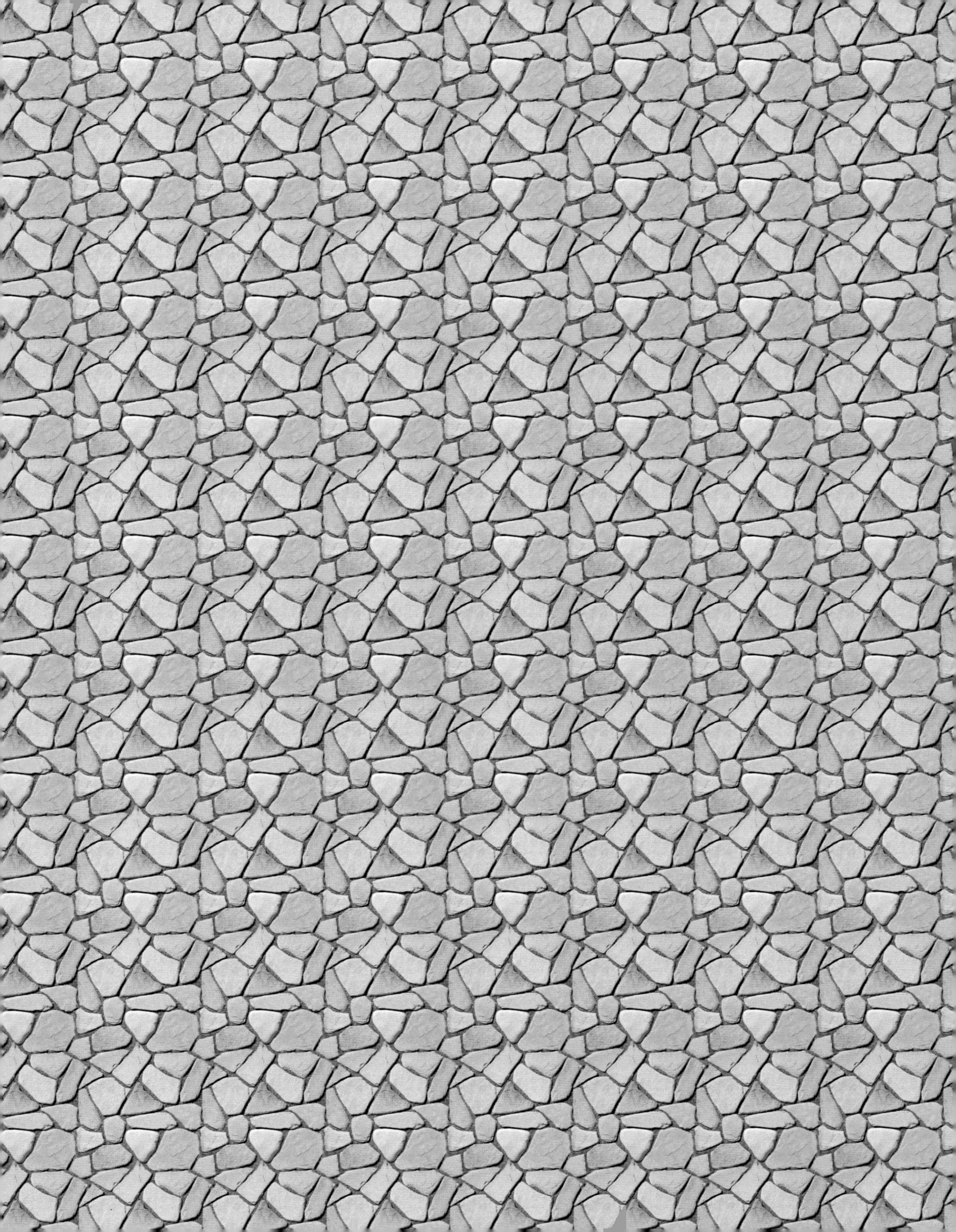

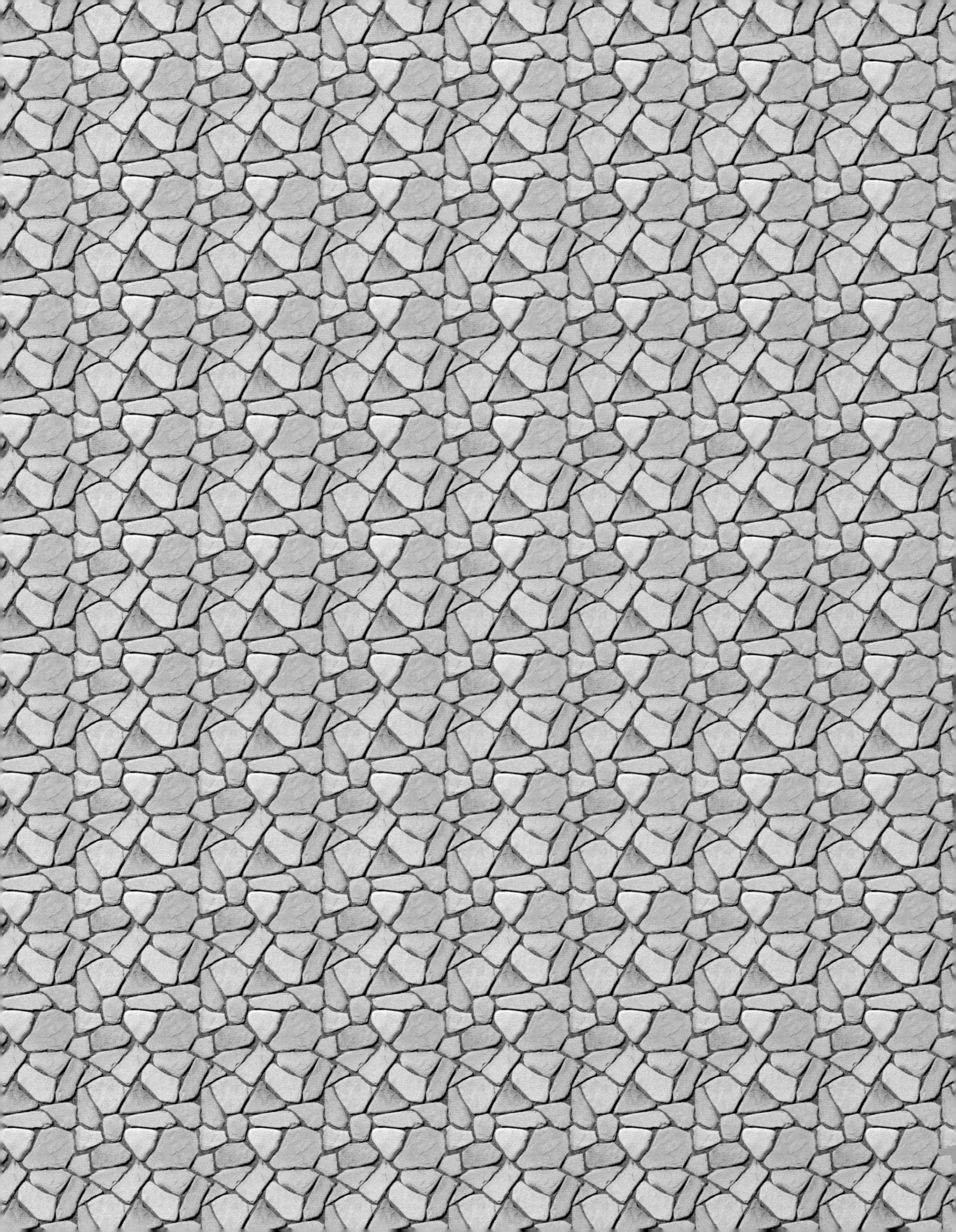

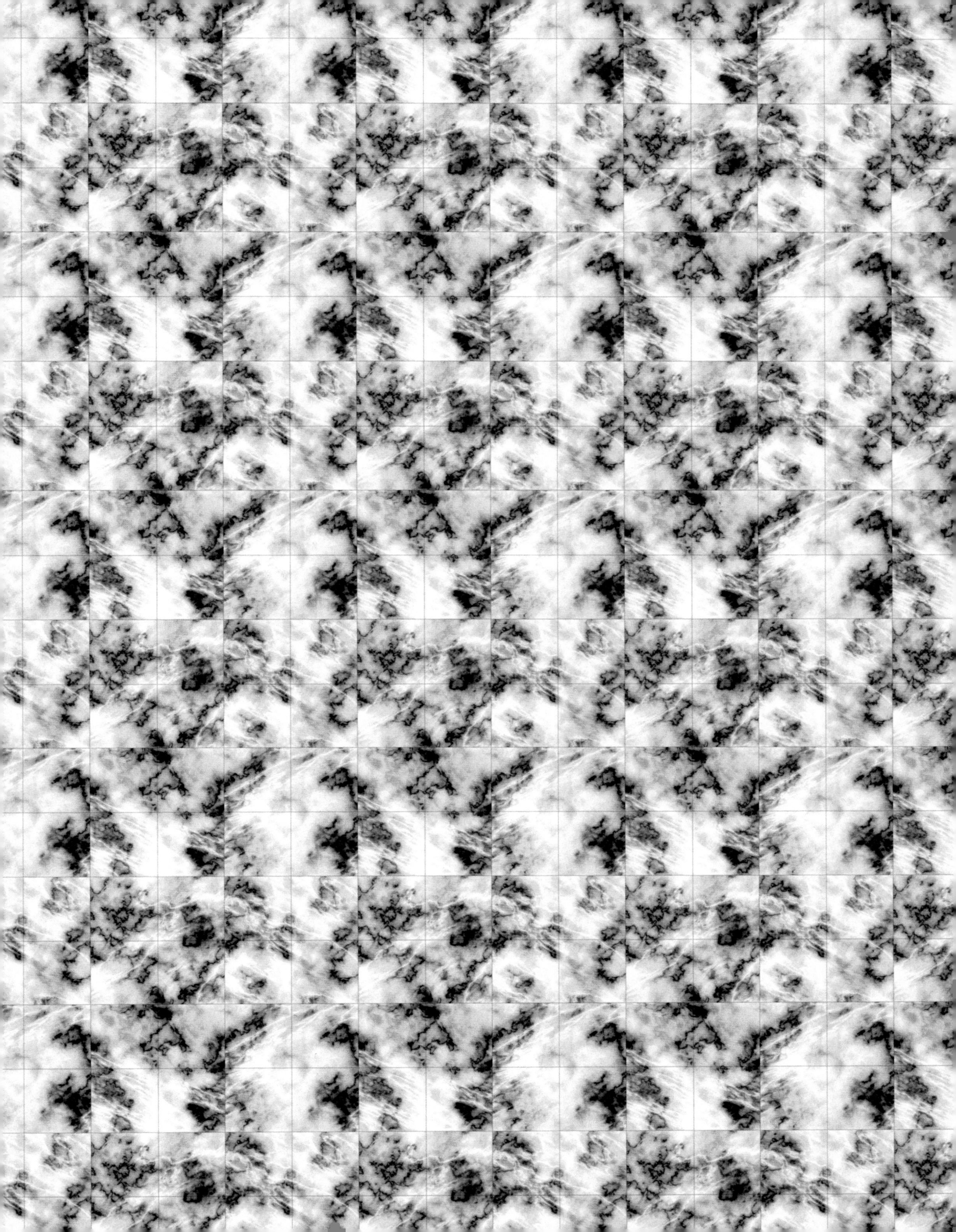

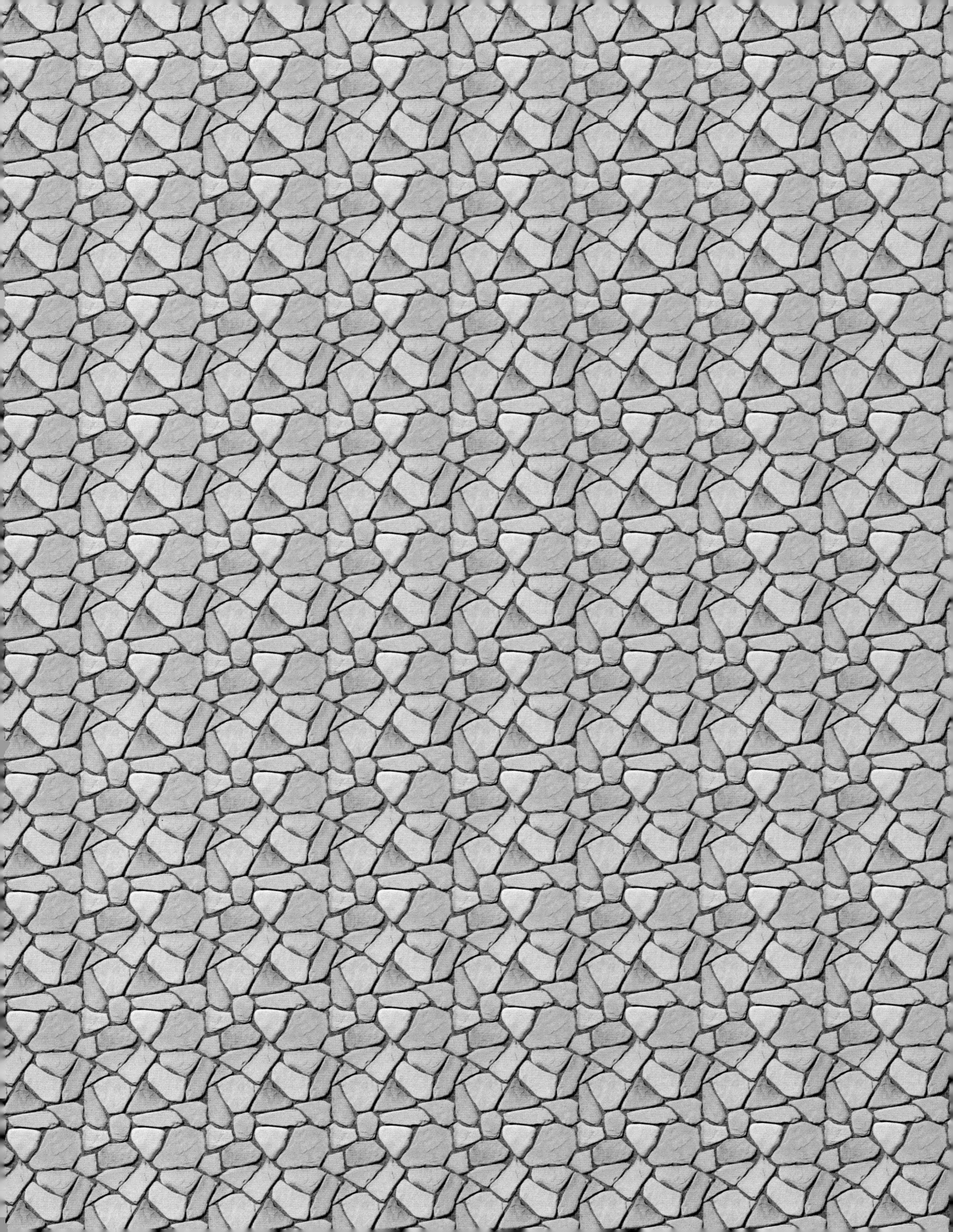

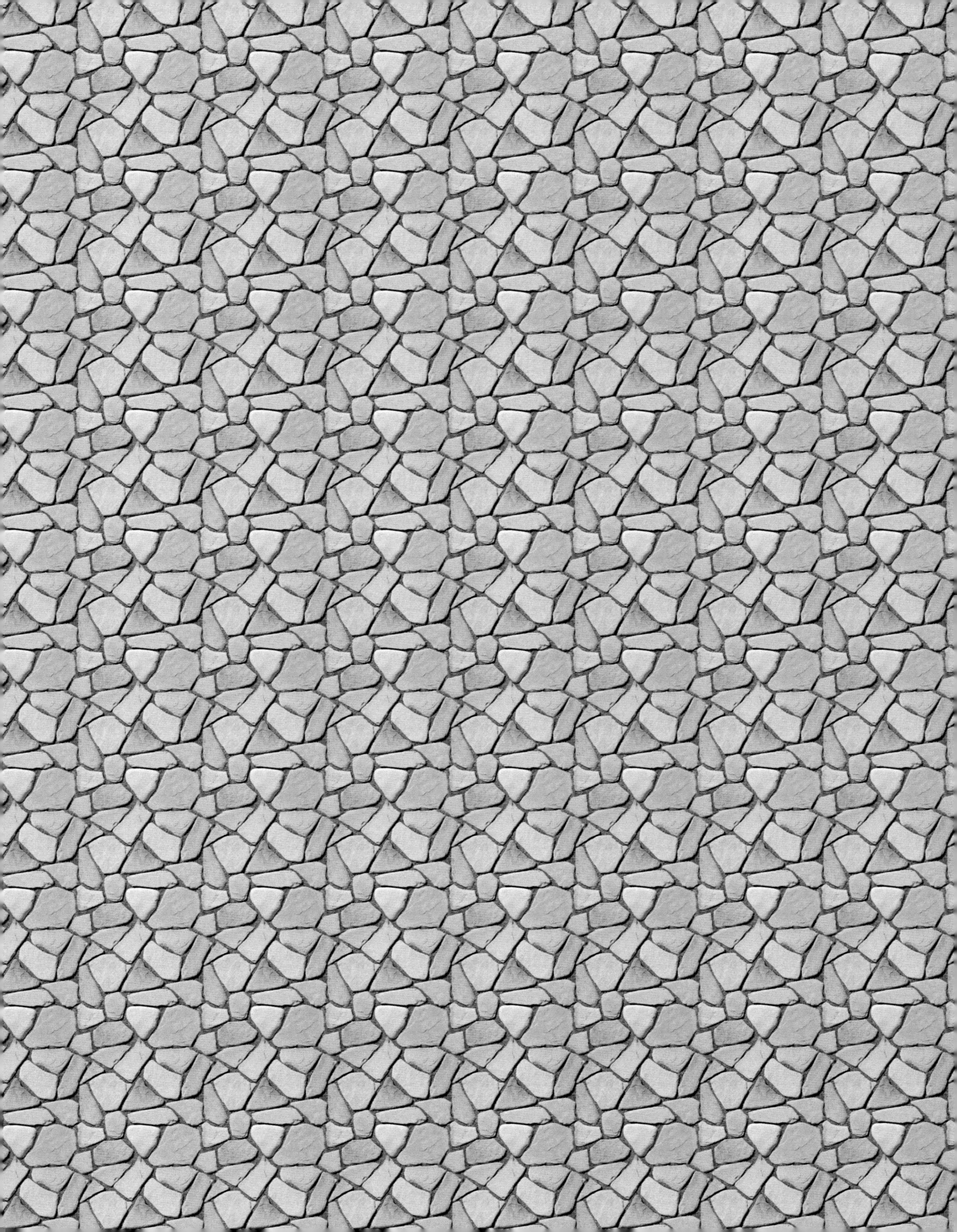

For more books of scrapbooking
and dollhouse papers search
"Anachronistic Textures"
on Amazon.

Made in the USA
Las Vegas, NV
28 November 2024

12832916R00038